Dedicated to the most complete person I have ever known.

M.D. Tophus

Exposing Glibness in Psychopathy.

Copyright ©. 2023. M.D. Tophus. All rights reserved

Hilphma Publications 2023. www.hilphmapublication.com

First Edition.

Germany.

The author has over 25 years of clinical experience in the healthcare field. Is cognisant of both DSM-5-TR (and previous versions) and ICD-11 (and previous versions) disorders and conditions; quality and safety improvement in healthcare; and healthcare education

Other M.D. Tophus publications available:

"Exercising Quality in Healthcare Service Provision: A Complex Care Workbook for All Healthcare Professionals." Germany: Hilphma Publications: 2022.

"Who is This Colleague?: Dangers of the Healthcare Profession, and beyond. An Interview Guide for Recruitment, Performance Appraisal and Post-Adverse Events." Germany: Hilphma Publications: 2022.

"Think on your Feet: Those Who Can. For the Consummate Healthcare Professional." Germany: Hilphma Publications: 2022.

"The Unfortunate Healthcare Treater, The Hapless Healthcare Therapist: Narcissistic and Borderline Personality Disorder clients. The Grit." Germany: Hilphma Publications: 2022.

"Victims of Crime: Introduction to Forensic Challenges in Healthcare." Germany: Hilphma Publications: 2022.

"The A to Z of Workplace Bullying: For the Healthcare Professional and Beyond." Germany: Hilphma Publications: 2022.

"Trauma United, Life Defined. A Healthcare Tool for Professionals Across the Globe." Germany: Hilphma Publications: 2022.

"Reflective Thinking: the True Healthcare Tool." Germany: Hilphma Publications: 2022.

"Burnout in Healthcare." Germany: Hilphma Publications: 2022.

"Reasonable Resilience in Workplaces and Healthcare Work." Germany: Hilphma Publications: 2022.

"The Psychological Impacts of Labelling and Failure to Diagnose." Germany: Hilphma Publications: 2022.

"The Controversy of the Remorseless and Unempathic Healthcare Worker."
Germany: Hilphma Publications: 2023.

"Attitudinal and Personality Traits in the Individual and Healthcare."
Germany: Hilphma Publications: 2023.

"Gaslighting."
Germany: Hilphma Publications: 2023.

"The Gaslighting Victims' Questionnaire (GVQ) and GVQ- Short form"
Germany: Hilphma Publications: 2023.

CONTENTS

Disturbingly, the classic psychopath is described as "embodying the concept of a well-adjusted, happy person" (1a).

Glibness is an essential component of psychopathy and is the primary focus in this publication.

Effective understanding of glibness can enhance appreciation of its significance in psychopathy, sociopathy, and antisocial personality disorder. Glibness, some may also argue, is a key to the individual's (of focus) contained (and often camouflaged) history.

Dangers of glibness extend to the exposition of a deranged individual who will stop at nothing to achieve their needs (which are actually indeed their 'wants').

Impacts of glibness, especially upon those around the glib, are so extensive that it becomes utterly perilous- on many levels- not the least, the emotional and psychological impacts.

Developmental stages of glibness (for instance, conduct disorder, or proof of multiple significant antisocial activities in pre, and intra, teen years), are often much more complicated.
The undetectability factor must be comprehended intelligently. When one is so impressively manipulative (often at a very early age), then others' observance and recognition of antisocial personality symptoms (and indeed psychopathy) often become obsolete, along with identification of additional binding symptoms (such as, callousness and unemotionality).

Profiling of glibness, integrates anti-social personality disorder- as considered the overriding term for both psychopathy, and sociopathy, as with:
Thaddeus (a pseudonym), who is an individual who presents with glibness/psychopathy. His particulars run through, from the childhood section through to the adulthood section of this book, as exemplification (and for ease of understanding and cross-relevancy), in support of the surrounding facts exposed.

Assessment of the glib- as the psychopath, involves multiple essential resources which are readily accessable, and assist in de-mystifying the particularly necessary identifiable components of glibness/psychopathy.

There are a comprehensive set of questions featured which substantially aid in fully realising the information detailed.

This publication comprises a thorough explanation of glibness/psychopathy, a subject of which has not been tackled in the mainstream.
It incorporates the indicators of glibness/psychopathy; how glibness is of such focussed importance; glibness and its direct relationship with psychopathy, sociopathy, and antisocial personality disorder; childhood, adolescence, and adulthood (including profiling for each) glibness/psychopathy; workplace glibness (psychopathy); and, assessment of glibness/psychopathy.
A comprehensive set of questions feature at the end of the publication in order to facilitate the reader, as necessarily inclusive.

There are several additional resources which may assist the reader in furthering their knowledge of glibness and psychopathy.

Including,

M.D. Tophus':

" Who is This Colleague?: Dangers of the Healthcare Profession, and beyond. An Interview Guide for Recruitment, Performance Appraisal and Post-Adverse Events."

and

"Gaslighting."

WHAT is GLIBNESS?

Glibness is defined as: "the quality of being easily fluent, especially in a way that is thoughtless, superficial, or insincere" (1b).

To be glib, is: "...showing little forethought or preparation (offhand)... marked by ease and informality (nonchalant).... lacking depth and substance (superficial) (2)

It is: "..marked by ease and fluency in speaking or writing often to the point of being insincere or deceitful...archaic: smooth, slippery" (2).

Synonymous with arrogance and smugness, <u>the glib</u> possesses: excessive pride in self; extreme self-satisfaction; beyond confidence; an absolute belief that they are far better than others and are unashamed about displaying it; and, disingenuousness.

They are deceptive, duplicitous, slick, flippant, superficial, charming, verbose, insincere, facile, and parasitic.

Their tactics place others in emotional, psychological, and sometimes- physical, danger.

Glibness incorporates a number of psychopathic traits.

Glibness- it is argued- is a product of multiple key factors: namely, superficial charm and "good 'intelligence'; absence of nervousness..; untruthfulness and insincerity; lack of remorse and shame; inadequately motivated antisocial behav or; pathological egocentricity and incapacity for love; general poverty of major affective reactions; unresponsiveness in general interpersonal relations. (3)

The Glibness categories below are proposed, in the realm of the successful psychopath classification (that is: ability to function and maintain self in mainstream society, with their attitudes, actions and behaviors generally accepted by others as fitting within social norms):

<u>DISCRETE GLIBNESS:</u> this glib has a high level of self-awareness; all glibs can read others very quickly and adapt, however- with the discrete glib- the effort is made to not just be charming and incredibly likeable, but to pursue a reputation of sincerity, genuineness, and empathy.

The <u>INDISCRETE GLIB</u> has (or chooses to have): tangible, or readable, glibness; less self-regulatory powers, or less impulse control, than the discrete glib; they continue to use charm and affability to pursue their objectives, but also have a 'take me as I am' attitude in combination, it can present as overt glibness or naively be reinterpreted as overconfidence.

<u>MORE TYPICAL OF INDISCRETE MALE GLIBNESS.:</u>

Underhanded 'ball curves', double speak, one-upmanship, obvious revenge tactics, manipulation, humiliation via nicety, domination via communication style, untrustworthiness, unreliability, and smooth talking.

The connector between indiscrete male and female glib expressions is the identical view to exploitation of ideas and people.

INDICATORS of GLIBNESS

Psychopathy cannot necessarily be categorised into neat boxes, each psychopath expresses their traits in different ways, and indeed has different degrees of intensity regarding certain traits. There are commonalities- which exist (typically in the successful principal psychopath), for instance, masked glibness (and to re-iterate) with directly associated superficial charm.

In regards to, fearlessness, disinhibition, and boldness, within interpersonal domains of psychopathy- these facets culminate to represent glibness (surface charm, and underlying callousness and unemotionality).

Pathological boldness involves having minimal levels of anxiety, immunity to stressors, fearlessness, reduced emotional reactivity, maximal attention-seeking behaviors, numbness to the concept of punitive measures, and social gregariousness.

So, if boldness/fearlessness (including glibness) is the predominating feature, it:

1/ does not mean that other elements are missing (they may just be very well hidden in high functioning successful psychopaths) and,

2/ it may represent a continuum of behaviors (often secreted from others) as opposed to being seperable from other facets (like e.g. impulsivity) and,

3/ may be indicative of a successful or adaptive sociopathy or emotionally stable psychopathy type

The glib is quintessentially, a: successful psychopath. Although he/she may be considered blessed with the gift of the gab, and appear to function socially and interpersonally, they use their exceptionally rehearsed skills to convince, lure, and assume control over situations and people. The successful psychopath usually has good to high levels of intelligence, ability to read others instantly, and possesses capacity for self-regulation (control over outward displays of aggression, impulsivity).

In particular, they cultivate their psychopathy fuelled manipulative techniques to the presentation of self as charismatic.

Charisma is: "compelling attractiveness or charm that can inspire devotion in others" (4) and "a special power that some people have naturally that makes them able to influence other people and attract their attention and admiration" (5).

It is "a personal magic of leadership arousing special popular loyalty or enthusiasm for a public figure.."; "a special magnetic charm or appeal" (6)

That is, charisma is used to deceive, control, and exploit, under a guise of morality and insightful affinity with others.

The information featured below, following the 'versus', is naturally the true glib behavior. The fact that the glib possesses such prowess at deceiving others is a testament to their enduring commitment and determination to get what they want regardless of the chosen methods.

Charisma and how sense of Entitlement is hidden, and the glib's cultivated perceptions, reinterpreted by others, as:

- SUPREMELY CONFIDENT versus narcissistic;

- genuinely CHARMING versus superficial charm;

- GENIUS or of gifted status;

- SOPHISTICATED;

- used to ACHIEVING maximally;

- admirably ASSERTIVE;

- highly LIKEABLE

- a GO-GETTER;

- already in a position of POWER where it is accepted or expected;

- INTERESTING, FASCINATING versus power hungry or dangerous;

- excellent LEADERSHIP QUALITIES;

- RESPONSIBLE and RELIABLE versus ownership or demanding acquiescence;

- reinforcement of aforementioned factors by others (that's just him/her).

How Callousness is hidden via the glib cultivating perceptions:

- STOICISM and SELF-REGULATORY emotional expression versus cruelty of thought and hidden cruel decision making and actions;

- PRAGMATIC approach to life versus absolute disregard for others' feelings;

- TASK FOCUSSED versus where problems present themselves (which involve impact on others);

- focussed on SELF-REFLECTION versus absence of true displays of empathy;

- LIFE HARDENED versus cold-heartedness;

At first, the glib presents as 'one with you'; understands you completely; appears to be sharing inside jokes one to one in a playful, ingratiating way; is clever, structured, and strategic; makes you feel like the centre of the universe; and seems eternally affable.

However,

looking under the surface, these are some of the behaviors which one discovers:

- secretive looks one to one- to imply threats toward you- but is invariably unproveable to others;

- reflects back spoken words as feigned positive affirmation of others to meet own needs;

- cleverly winds in own achievements (in discussions);

- takes credit for others' achievements;

- has awareness of being watched, observed, and considers it like a test which they often convincingly pass;

- body language seems rehearsed and prone to mimicry to ingratiate self, but use of pre-planned open body language, micro-expressions, gestures, and mannerisms, are consistently evident;

- everything is a performance to advance reputation, needs, plans, public persona/ profile;

- manipulation of others' words to own advantage;

- the glib brings others around to his/her conclusions and beliefs;

- smug knowingness which is perceived as only understood by the privileged/ chosen few;

- structured hand gestures to denote desire to communicate and connect with others;

- encourages camraderie, partnership and opportunity of thought- but with contextual underpinnings;

- mirrors others to create connection, reliance- with view to control;

- modelling versus meeting others half way;

- is relentlessly ambitious;

- on-demand blushing (when caught out, to communicate humility);

- pre-planned witty comments;

- contrived vulnerability;

- clarification versus ownership of culpability/accountability;

- upon being revealed as not the perfect person they appear to be, the bait and switch technique is used (the glib will admit to perpetrating harm at the same time as stating that they witnessed harm- implicating others, and minimising their own accountability);

- masks aggression with perceptive leaking and prescriptive advice;

- externalises regret as generalised, and globalised, in nature;

- evasive upon being questioned, thence seeks accolades for apparent honesty (which are invariably lies);

- disclosure, in the name of solidarity, in response to unlawful conduct- thus, implicating all in the group;

- justification for unlawful actions with no regret nor guilt owned;

- communication of moral thought, perception, and responsibility, is contingent upon legalities pertaining to the glib;

- learned lessons are cited as a generic response- distanced emotions;

- inability to grasp ethical and moral responsibility as their own- typically broadening it to the wider community as responsible;

- secrecy is often maintained via usage of metaphors- cited as justified disclosure of specifics regarding hidden agendas.

How Unemotionality is hidden via the glib cultivating perceptions:

- SELF-CONTAINED versus aloof;

- warped sense of HUMOR versus complete ambivalence toward others;

- TARGETTED RESPONSES versus apathetic;

- HUMBLE versus devoid of care;

- CALM versus absolute immunity to stress/inappropriate fearlessness;

- PERSONABLE versus invading personal space.

How Insincerity is hidden via the glib cultivating perceptions:

- WARM versus faking interest;

- GREGARIOUS versus sycophantic;

- team member INCLUSIVE versus disloyal;

- SELF-ANALYTICAL versus selfish;

- PRIDE in self and accomplishments versus feelings of superiority.

<u>**How Deception is hidden via the glib cultivating perceptions:**</u>

- <u>**DIPLOMATIC versus evasive;**</u>

- <u>**CREATIVE THINKER versus outright liar;**</u>

- <u>**ENTERTAINING versus confabulator;**</u>

- <u>**has an ANSWER for everything versus non-disclosure about guilt;**</u>

- <u>**STRAIGHT TALKER versus gaslighting;**</u>

- <u>**CONFLICT RESOLVER versus propagating lies;**</u>

- <u>**SHREWD versus slippery.**</u>

<u>**How Duplicity is hidden via the glib cultivating perceptions:**</u>

- <u>**SUPPORTIVE of others' ideas versus theft of concepts;**</u>

- <u>**OUTSPOKEN versus splitting behaviors;**</u>

- <u>**INTELLECTUAL versus cunning;**</u>

- <u>**PLAYFUL versus undercutting;**</u>

- <u>**FINANCIALLY SAVVY versus perversely incentivised;**</u>

- <u>**helpfully INSTRUCTIONAL versus analogises to manipulate others' emotions;**</u>

- <u>**BENEVOLENT versus malicious;**</u>

- <u>**CONTEMPLATIVE and measured versus lack of remorse.**</u>

<u>**How Manipulation is hidden via the glib cultivating perceptions:**</u>

- **<u>SOCIAL PROWESS versus egocentricity;</u>**

- **<u>PRESCRIPTIVE APPROACH versus threatening;</u>**

- **<u>FLATTERING versus love-bombing;</u>**

- **<u>PHILOSOPHICAL versus projection of blame;</u>**

- **<u>FACT FOCUSSED versus twisting and denigrating others' words and ideas;</u>**

- **<u>SYMPATHETIC versus honing in on vulnerabilities;</u>**

- **<u>great ORATOR versus machiavellian controller;</u>**

- **<u>TRUSTWORTHY versus a friendly (cheshire cat style) schemer;</u>**

- **<u>NATURAL LEADER versus no respect for authority</u>**.

Glibness combines multiple traits within (antisocial, sociopathic and) psychopathic continua.

Importantly, "one third of those who are diagnosed with antisocial personality disorder meet criteria for psychopathy" (7).

There is a clear interrelationship between glibness and the individual components of antisocial personality disorder (for instance, antagonism, and disinhibition).

Moreover, glibness in a high functioning successful principal psychopath, may not be tangibly evident in an individual -for years- pre-assessment.

Therefore emphasising the importance of identifying glibness on a pre-pathological diagnostic level, given the insidious, machiavellian nature of the glib and the significant impacts this can have upon others.

Ultimately, each characteristic feeds the other. One cannot be truly glib without callousness, grandiosity, and manipulativeness.

So too, confabulation (which essentially involve lies, creation of stories and a false persona to achieve what he/she wants). These are all part of the glibness narrative.

Taking advantage of others, and complete inconsideration when pushed about other's feelings, a charm offensive presents along with feigned empathy, and is forever present within the glib (psychopath). However, their true colours are detectable upon informed curiosity by others (and adequate use of intuition).

Exploitation and arrogance is standard within these individuals, as with a predatory and parasitic approach toward others, circumstances, and environments.

Positive impression management (PIM) is a form of representation of self. The person utilises power over others to present a certain image, to create perceptions that are favorable. This is the glib's modus operandi. It is well known to be used by those with significant traits of psychopathy (glibness with primary focus upon tactics of manipulation techniques and surface charm).

Power and dominance driven, the glib consistently compels others to subscribe to their charm ridden ideas, and ideals.

Along with demands, they manipulate significant others (either in the workplace or personal life) into a false sense of security, feeling assured that the glib is trustworthy, honest, and morally sound.

They (the glib) are neverthelesss, empty inside, seeking power at all costs, are engulfed by the need for greed, and always have sinister motives.
They create a fascinating persona but at everyone else's peril.
Danger is an understatement, when entering their world.

Ultimately, the formulaic representation of some of the glib's characteristics, is:

boldness= fearlessness= dauntlessness= audacity= decimation (of others' character, and, psyche).

Anti-social personality disorder is often considered the umbrella term for sociopathy and psychopathy.

The differences between sociopathy and psychopathy are consistent with principal and secondary psychopathy definitions, as introduced in earlier pages of this publication.

To clearly delineate the particular aspects of glibness with psychopathy, the following is to be considered:

- **identity:** egocentrism; self-esteem is achieved via personal gain; pleasure or, power

- **self-direction:** goal setting based personal gratification; no prosocial internal standards; failure to conform (legally or) cultural based standards of ethical behavior

- **empathy:** complete lack of concern for other individuals; along with lack of remorse

- **intimacy:** inability for reciprocally intimate connections; exploitation as a primary way of relating to others; this incorporates use of deceit and coercion; along with

dominance or intimidation in order to control others

- **manipulativeness (a form of antagonism):** regular usage of subterfuge to influence
or control other individuals; use of glibness; seduction; charm; or, ingratiation as a
means to achieve pre-planned results

- **deceitfulness (antagonism):** dishonesty (and fraud based activity);

self-misrepresentation; exaggeration or confabulation upon describing events to others

- **callousness (antagonism):** nil concern for feelings or problems of other individuals

- **risk taking (a form of disinhibition):** thoughtless start of endeavours; lack of

concern for own limitations and reality denial of personal danger to own person

- **irresponsibility (disinhibition):** rejection of commitments or obligations; nil

realisation of promises and agreements

- *specification of psychopathic features (for instance, bold interpersonal style, lack of*

anxiety or fear, high attention seeking, social potency) provide further assistance in

accurate identification of psychopathy, and it is argued, its relationship with glibness

related characteristics (8)

<u>**The link of focus, between Glibness, narcissism, and psychopathy lies in the following descriptions:**</u>

> **Narcissism incorporates being completely self-entitled; a grandiose conceptualisation of self-importance, belief that one is superior to others; controlling of others; having deficits in regard for others; and, significant mistrust.**

> **Psychopathy involves unemotionality; callousness; constant manipulation; inability to experience feelings of guilt and remorse; being exploitatory; calculatively manipulative; having surface affect; and, extreme egocentricity.**

As detailed earlier, there is a significant proportion of anti-social personality disordered individuals who fit the diagnosis of psychopathy.

The binding of each is found in the expression (and these underpinnings) of glibness.

It is necessary to explain the specific differences between <u>the secondary and principal psychopath</u>. The former has the capacity to show loyalty, a desire (albeit fleeting) to empathise with others, at times- entertains the experience of remorse, and intimate feelings (and love) are pursued on a pseudo meaningul level.

Secondary psychopathy is considered to be on a continuum. Many fitting the description present with callousness/unemotionality features but display capability in recognising stressors as stressors, and can experience anxiety (they do not necessarily feel 'emotionally responsive deadness inside'). Some lean toward obvious risk taking.

Fearlessness, in particular, can provide a key to identifying type of psychopathy, with the principal (versus the secondary) psychopath experiencing fearlessness.
Both can possess glibness, however.

Here (regarding glibness), principal psychopathy is the focus. It is sometimes referred to as the classic, or prototypical, psychopath.

Generally, the glib is able to hide behind his/her fearlessness, verbosity, and high social functionality (especially being able to secrete true intent of their ideas and actions, which are fuelled by callousness etc).

Hereto:

"He or she, usually he, appears to be something he or she is not.
The prototypical psychopath makes an appealing first impression on others that conceals a darker and more affectively empty interior. The chameleon-like nature of the psychopath may be what makes this hybrid creature both interpersonally alluring and interpersonally dangerous (9)—alluring because he is charismatic, confident, and excitement seeking, and dangerous because he can lure us into a false sense of trust, as in the prototype of the confidence ("con") artist".(10)

Stress, anxiety, and fear along with intellectual deficiencies, are not expected issues in children and adolescents (nor adults) who present with (anti-social) glibness and manipulative behaviors.

These particular types of antisocial behaviors are often slow to be identified, as the child or adolescent, is considered to be assimilated.

Glibness which is realised via convincing, but on the surface charm, and disturbing self-centredness, remain present in childhood, adolescence, through to (and including) adulthood.
Even in childhood, the capacity for extensive manipulation, with often excellent verbal abilities, are everpresent.

Glibness can be a deciding factor in the case of later development of antisocial personality disorder (and psychopathy). The individual usually has good intelligence and can manipulate effectively whilst appearing normal and functioning socially.
Thus, being able to hide their pathology.

Callousness/unemotionality can manifest as meanness, especially in conduct disordered children (and adolescents).

It is important to comprehend the diagnostic components of conduct disorder (which is often a forerunner for antisocial personality disorder- psychopathy) and its interrelationship with glibness:

Relevant conduct disorder criteria, include: "often bullies, threatens, or intimidates others"; "has been physically cruel to people"; "often lies to obtain goods or favors or to avoid obligations (i.e., "cons" others)." (8)

Diagnostically, one must specify if the individual has limited prosocial emotions.

Glibness factors: shallow or deficient affect: "does not express feelings or show emotions to others, except in ways that seem shallow, insincere, or superficial (e.g., actions contradict the emotion displayed; can turn emotions "on" or "off" quickly) or when emotional expressions are used for gain (e.g., emotions displayed to manipulate or intimidate others)." (8)

Shallow or deficient affect, can also be accompanied by lack of remorse or guilt; and/or callousness- lack of empathy, in particular.

Further parameters of specification include: childhood-onset, adolescent-onset, or unspecified onset, types; and if mild, moderate, or severe.

Seperating out from considerations of immaturity, poor social skills, parenting style, societal or virtual desensitization, and stage of moral development, a child without the capacity to internally react to anothers' suffering is a concern on many levels.

3 year old Thaddeus had a predominance of glibness; though apparently kind to dogs, when his mother was injured on multiple occasions, he expressed pleasure with laughter and teasing behind closed doors- yet shallow, rehearsed communications of sadness about the situation to gain sympathy for self and redirect attention/become the centre of attention about the incidences- in front of others. Upon being cared for by others (even for a short time), Thaddeus made up stories that he had

been abused (hit, manhandled) with concomitant screaming, and subsequent evident cruelty expressed along with clear non-verbal communication of a 'haha' I'm getting you into trouble.

He enjoyed seeing significant others cry but attempted to guard enjoyment in front of witnesses.

A rapid behavioral progression ensued (in a matter of months) to honing convincing (but evidently shallow) affect, and affection, in addition to an ability to turn emotions on and off at a whim (whilst being able to maintain the emotion to optimise reaction, especially from adults, when opportunity presented itself).

Key points:

-no likewise modelling behaviors from significant others, nil identified mimicking of cruelty

-due to level of cunning (and ability to overpower)- perceived as intelligence by the primary parent, the aforementioned parent was unaccepting that the child was displaying concerning behaviors

When Thaddeus was 6 years old- he was affable, charming, with the gift of the gab, making targetted adults feel that they are the only person in the world that he trusts, confides in; flirtatious, and affectionate, with significant and non-significant adult females; and, he successfully initiated discussion, games, and appropriate expressions of emotion, re-enacting events in an adultified manner

-key indicators of glibness, and antisocial behaviors, identified (by caregivers), when the child believed he was not being observed, included psychological and physical cruelty toward other children. He was almost always able to provide a convincing reason for these behaviors, and negotiated advantageously to avoid punishment and exposure to outside significant others.

-the charm and verbal communications were (even at 6 years of age) propagated effectively- nevertheless, with those understanding of pathological childhood behaviors, with shallow affect

-he engaged in constant checking for reaction to judge successfulness of things said, when judged unsuccessful by Thaddeus, he displayed an ability to rapidly shift, and employ love-bombing, as a decoy

-he had an enduring adultified awareness as to how to remain unaccountable for any actions (such as cruelty, in appropriate or predatory behaviors)

-ultimately, Thaddeus (at this age) became effectively chameleon-like.

Lack of anxiety in children with conduct disorder, it is argued, is linked with lack of impulsivity.

As an 8 year old- Thaddeus via his natural cunning, manipulativeness, and secretiveness- upon realisation of opportunity- was able to shift instantly to a charm offensive (time and time again). That was along with his other traits (from the age of 3 years onward).

He also presented with:

-sophisticated communicative reasoning regarding reward and non-reward from parental figures

-ability to maintain secrecy, to the point of seperation,'life divisions (regardless of the high interactivity of significant parental figures)

-high effectiveness in using splitting behaviors between teachers, allied professionals, parental figures, and other

-surprisingly calm demeanour, with nil anxiety, even in emergency situations

-capacity for protracted chameleon-like mannerisms, personality features, actions and behaviors, consistent with the present company of others.

32

"Psychopathy in early adolescence uniquely predicts psychopathy in young adulthood even after controlling for race, family structure, SES, neighborhood, poor parenting, bad peers, impulsivity, intelligence, and previous delinquency, but there are other important variables left uncontrolled." (11)

Adolescents and youth presenting with psychopathic traits (and its interrelationship with glibness) are considered via:

"...the four-factor structure recently proposed by Hare (12). Three items assess an arrogant, deceitful interpersonal style (facet 1): superficial, grandiose, and deceitful; 3 items assess deficient affective experience (facet 2): lacks remorse, lacks empathy, and does not accept responsibility; 3 items assess an impulsive and irresponsible behavioral style (facet 3): impulsivity, lacks goals, and irresponsible; and 3 assess antisocial behavior (facet 4): poor behavioral controls, adolescent antisocial behavior, and adult antisocial behavior. " (11)

It must be noted that callous and unemotional traits are independently present regardless of positive or negative parenting practises.

At 14 years of age, Thaddeus fully engaged in perverse cruelty (synonymous with his life blood philosophy, enjoying immensely acts of cruelty, and the impacts- including verbal and non-verbal feedback/reactions from victims).

However, this was undertaken in secret.

He had the immense ability to instantly refocus, combined effectively with use of glibness factors.

This seemed to make Thaddeus an unstoppable, but yet seemingly socially functioning, force.

Glibness traits associated with antisocial personality (disorder), and with conduct disorder (in earlier life), involve contravention and fracturing of the core natural rights of other individuals or, defying commonly accepted standards of society.

By the time that Thaddeus was 17 years of age-(post-conduct disorder into anti-social personality disorder/sociopathy/psychopathy diagnostic time period), he had developed a stunning capability to 'put one over' anyone who crossed his path.

From family members, to friends, to part-time workmates, acquaintances, and strangers, there was no-one that he could not conquer with his well-honed verbal and behavioral style of interacting.

Good to high intelligence as linked with high functioning verbal skills; capacity to analyse situations; logic; and versatility in interpersonal functioning, which involves grandiosity and manipulation, are predominant features of glibness.

The glib powered by egocentricity, and indeed narcissistic traits, is whetted to utilise and enhance this high functionality:

"Individuals with antisocial personality disorder frequently lack empathy and tend to be callous, cynical, and contemptuous of the feelings, rights, and sufferings of others. They may have an inflated and arrogant self-appraisal (e.g., feel that ordinary work is beneath them or lack a realistic concern about their current problems or their future) and may be excessively opinionated, self-assured, or cocky." (8)

In early adulthood (ages 18 to 30 years), Thaddeus excelled in his life pursuits. He was suspected (by some) as disingenuous, but never called out on it.

He had achieved (what most would term) the pinnacle of success in his professional life.

His personal life was picture perfect, but without honesty, substance, and depth of intimacy.

He was out totally for himself, and everyone very close to him (at least, life proximally) intuitively knew it, but were unable to state it, nor reason with someone (with him) who was devoid of the normal spectrum of human emotions and morality.

In effect, they were too scared (yes, of him- but more of how he may react- in forms of revenge, disloyalty, betrayal, deceit and subterfuge).

Nevertheless, to those outside his personal sphere, he remained viewed as relentlessly charming and charismatic.

"Some antisocial individuals may display a glib, superficial charm and can be quite voluble and verbally facile (e.g., using technical terms or jargon that might impress someone who is unfamiliar with the topic).

Lack of empathy, inflated self-appraisal, and superficial charm are features that have been commonly included in traditional conceptions of psychopathy that may be particularly distinguishing of the disorder" (8)

Upon reaching middle adulthood (31 to 50 years of age), Thaddeus had learned that his glibness was a successful vehicle to anything in which he chose to focus and succeed.

Power over others was his ultimate aim, and he was achieving this in leaps and bounds.

Thaddeus, in older adulthood (age 51 years onward), appeared to mellow slightly in his core glibness.

Thaddeus had always known that he was vastly different from other people, that his actions, behaviors, mannerisms, and communications, were 'all show' to gratify his own needs and wants.

He felt that he had succeeded, and although he craved more and more success and power, he discovered that the fuel which enabled this was becoming less and less.

He wanted to take a break from this, albeit temporarily.

Although his commitment to subterfuge, power, success, and betrayal, was never ending, he (for the first time in his life) became unsure as to whether his energy resources would see this out.

He continued to think that honesty, true expressions of intimacy, loyalty and empathy, represented stupidity and weakness, nevertheless he wondered if there may be something more to life.

GLIBNESS in the WORKPLACE

In some workplaces, overt, and suspected (covert), glibness and other psychopathic traits (without impulsivity) are considered attractive qualities- especially when a company is seeking to employ a manager, leader, or a mid to high level employee- when the company is in turmoil or in the midst of significant workplace changes.

Termed 'corporate psychopathy', it is often reinforced by management, and leaders in a variety of work environments.

This phenomenon is called corporate psychopathy because it is based on the assumption that the corporate environment positively selects for psychopathic features, especially in top stewardship.

Power, prestige, accolades, and recompense, are at the core of a glib's (psychopath's) attraction to specific types of work settings.

These include, workplace cultures which encourage and reward competitiveness, provide plentiful financial advantages, demand immediacy (versus long-term work planning), and have positive expectations regarding the employee's charisma.

The glib's ability to:

thrive on chaos; be creative; maintain their composure (unstressed) during times of workplace challenges; employ constant strategic cognitions and behaviors; and possessing supreme confidence unabated, is often highly valued by upper echelons (versus their immediate co-workers).

Excellent communication skills is also considered a desirable quality when accompanied by the previously mentioned features.

If impressively delineative, 'on face value' working style is valued (by the corporation) more strongly **than** that of productivity, exemplary leadership skills, and beyond satisfactory functioning within teams. Thence, the glib (psychopath) is more easily promoted to a higher position.

Needless to state, the experiences of a glib's (psychopath's) co-worker typically differs greatly from upper management.

The colleague (whether they be on the same work level, or be managed by the glib) witnesses and suffers the impacts of the glib's risk-taking and unethical decision making, their bullying tactics, and threats.

Specifically, one must examine the different stages and factors involving admittance of a glib/psychopath into a company:

The recruitment stage involves necessity of insight by the recruiter. Otherwise, the recruiter will yield to the following strategic manoeuvres of the glib/psychopath:

charm; unbreakable confidence; extremely engaging, complimentary and humorous; exceptional powers of persuasion; perfection of mannerism and gestures; and overall, so impressive that one can hardly believe the person sitting before you is real- but they are ultimately believed to be perfect for the position.

Furthermore, in the realm of competitiveness, there is frequently "easier recruitment of malicious minded individuals when the concept of competition is introduced (alibi)" (13)

A fast-tracked career climb thence <u>ensues.</u>

That is, with use of:

no scruples; nil loyalty to colleagues, no fairness as in who was there first or who is next in line for a promotion; joy in having people demoted, sacked, or suspended; merciless manipulation; incessant socialising, charming and lying their way up the ladder- in rapid progression almost immediately; and, befriending and ingratiating themselves with upper echelons in any way that they can.

Theft of ideas; emotional (or other) bribery so that co-workers perform the work tasks for them; and, mimicry of high achievers (their own capacity for inventive and original concepts and work production is limited) occurs very quickly <u>following the orientation phase</u> of employment.

Elimination of any competitive colleagues; achieving higher status and appearance of high work productivity; splitting between colleagues and teams; creation of a toxic work culture; and, use of tactics, which create an environment where co-workers (instead of the guilty) seem to constantly fail, leads to further cunning strategies.

Such as,

character assassination (via gossip, inuendo, and outright fabrication of truths); and, gaslighting:

"Thus, corporate/institutional/workplace gaslighting (with 'corporate/workplace stockholm syndrome' type symptoms) often incorporates: -identification with the captor (manager, colleague) whilst in a hostage like situation (entrapped employee, co-worker) and doubting one's own (V of G's) sense of reality and perception of negative events, which are recurrent" (14)

To assist in minimising chances of a glib/psychopath being employed, a myriad of checks must be utilised as standard protocol before (and immediately following) the recruitment interview. So too, a formulated interview guide (as featured comprehensively in reference 15).

To exemplify focus upon glibness, within one area of work:

HEALTHCARE WORKPLACE ASSESSMENT of GLIBNESS

Suffice to state, one does not want a pathological glib in one's work environment:

"Does the respondent laugh inappropriately at (or 'make light of') serious scenarios or events presented?

Does he/she have indifference to patient suffering?

Which behaviours, during the interview, indicate to you (if any) that the applicant is purposefully haphazard in their attitude to diagnosing, treating, and caring, for their potential/current patients?

Does he/she seem superficial, or thoughtless, in their attitudes to healthcare/patient care?

How sincere is the interviewee?

-does he/she appear to have standard answers which 'roll off the tongue' , with no meaningfulness?

-does she/he appear pleased with their responses regardless of verbal/non-verbal feedback of interviewer/s?

Does the interviewee seem unprepared, but 'happy to wing it'?

-are there 'in your face', 'tough luck' reactions to the interviewer/s?

Are your (as an interviewer) suspicions about glibness supported by paperwork (for example, curriculum vitae, application material)?

Does the respondent reduce questions by giving smooth, oversimplified answers?

Interviewer's guide: Further information potentially indicative of Glibness: clinical and workplace ambivalence (maverick attitude to responsibilities and care of patients), sadistic humour (which is meaningful and crosses over to clinical work), pride in 'not playing by the rules' (in violation of accepted medical knowledge, or practices)" (15)

ASSESSMENT of GLIBNESS

Given that glibness is representative of psychopathy traits, it is essential for eligible individuals to be comprehensively assessed.

The following assessment measures are an example of some with the most relevancy.

The measures are categorised into: adulthood (below); adolescent/youth; and, childhood (the assessment specific to workplace environments features earlier in this resource).

<u>**ADULTHOOD TESTS:**</u>

The PSYCHOPATHIC PERSONALITY INVENTORY-REVISED (PPI-R)

-154 items

-8 scales:

   -Machiavellian Egocentricity;

   -Social Influence;

   -Fearlessness;

   -Rebellious Nonconformity;

   -Carefree Nonplanfulness;

   -Blame Externalization;

   -Stress Immunity; and

   -Cold-heartedness

-Incorporates the approach that psychopathy covaries from individual to individual.

(10).

<u>TRIARCHIC PSYCHOPATHY MEASURE</u> (TriPM)

-58-item self-report inventory

-it is based on an open construct model of psychopathy

-assesses:

- -Boldness

- -Meanness

- -Disinhibition

via 3 subscales.

The TriPM Boldness scale measures:

-pre-disposition toward fearlessness (resiliency, self-confidence, and optimism)

-interpersonal behavior (persuasiveness, social assurance, and that of
 dominance)

-venturesomeness (courage, thrill seeking, and tolerance of uncertainty)

-charm

The TriPM Meanness scale assesses:

-callousness

-unemotionality

-exploitativeness

The TriPM Disinhibition scale examines:

-planful control

-irresponsibility

-alienation

-dependability

-impatient urgency

-boredom proneness

-problematic impulsivity

-fraud

-theft

(16).

The PSYCHOPATHY RESEMBLANCE INDEX (NEO PRI)

-120 items

- it examines 30 personality areas incorporating the big five personality domains:

-neuroticism

-extraversion

-openness to experience

-conscientiousness

-agreeableness.

There is a NEO PRI- Revised version available (11).

The Psychopathy Check List- Revised (PCL-R)

-20 items

-involves a semi-structured interview

-measures:

- emotional detachment

- antisocial behavior

-It examines areas, including:

-glibness/superficial charm;

-grandiose sense of self-worth;

-need for stimulation;

-pathological lying;

-cunning/manipulative;

-lack of remorse or guilt;

-shallow affect;

-callous/lack of empathy;

-parasitic lifestyle;

-poor behavioral controls;

-promiscuous sexual behavior;

-early behavior problems;

-lack of realistic goals;

-impulsivity;

-irresponsibility;

-failure to accept responsibility;

-many short-term relationships;

-juvenile delinquency;

-revocation of conditional release;

-criminal versatility.

(17a).

-20 items

-self-report

-measures:

-affective responsiveness;

-cognitive responsiveness;

-interpersonal manipulation;

-egocentricity

(17b).

ADOLESCENT TESTS

Antisocial Process Screening Device (APSD)

-20 items

-different versions: children, parents, teachers

-4 to 18 years

- 3 subscales:

  -narcissism,

  -impulsiveness,

  -callous unemotional

  (18).

Psychopathy Check List- Youth Version (PCL-YV)

-20 items

-13+ years (12-15 years generally used)

-scales measure the following areas:

  -interpersonal,

  -affective,

  -deviancy

  (19).

<h2 style="text-align:center;"><u>Youth Psychopathic Traits Inventory (YPI)</u></h2>

-50 item self-report

-12 years and over eligibility

- it has 10 scales:

    -dishonest charm

    -grandiosity

    -lying

    -manipulation

    -remorselessness

    -callousness

    -unemotionality

    -impulsiveness

    -irresponsibility

    -thrill seeking.

    (20)

CHILDHOOD TESTS

The Child Problematic Traits Inventory (CPTI)

-28 items

- it assesses psychopathic (personality) traits

- ages 3 to 12 years' eligibility

(21).

Child Psychopathy Scale- and Revised/Modified version (CPS, and CPS-R/mCPS)

-41 items (original); modified version 55 items:

-12 to 18 years (though possible use for younger ages)

-Areas of assessment include:

- -Glibness
- -Untruthfulness
- -Manipulation
- -Lack of guilt
- -Callousness
- -Poverty of affect
- -Failure to accept responsibility
- -Boredom (susceptability to)

-Parasitic (lifestyle)

-Planning (lack thereof)

-Impulse control (impulsiveness)

-Unreliability

-Behavioral control (dysfunction/dyscontrol)

(22).

Please see page 41 for workplace (healthcare) assessment of glibness.

ABBREVIATIONS

ASB: Anti-Social Behaviors

ASPD: Anti-Social Personality Disorder

ASPD: Anti-Social Process Screening Device (Frick)

CPS: Child Psychopathy Scale (Lynam)

CU: Callous/Unemotional traits

e.g.: exempli gratia/ for example

etc: etcetera

i.e.: id est/ that is

PCL-R: Psychopathy Check List- Revised (Hare)4

PIM: Positive Impression Management (linked to theory and scale)

PPI-R: Psychopathy Personality Inventory (?Lilienfeld)

SES: Social Economic Status

TriPM: Triarchic Psychopathy Measure

V of G: Victims of Gaslighting

1/ How can one define 'glibness'?

2/ What is synonymous with smugness and arrogance?

3/ True or false: the glib is typically ingenuous.

4/ Name 5 other characteristics of the glib.

5/ Provide an example which you believe indicates a glib placing

someone in physical danger.

6/ Why is glibness an element of psychopathy?

7/ Describe 3 key factors based on Cleckley.

8/ What is a successful psychopath?

9/ Which type of glib typically pursues a reputation of sincerity?

10/ Which other elements do they pursue?

11/ Which type of glib has more difficulty with self-regulation?

12/ Explain glibness and 'take me as I am'.

13/ Give 3 examples which typify male glibness.

14/ Provide 2 examples by which one may identify a female glib.

15/ What is the connector between male and female glibness?

16/ Can psychopathy be fitted into neat boxes?

   Please explain your answer.

17/ What is a commonality within psychopathy?

18/ Which interpersonal domains represent glibness?

19/ What does pathological boldness involve?

20/ Complete the following: with boldness/fearlessness (including glibness) present, in relation to psychopathy:

a) all other elements are missing

b) often secreted behaviors from others occur

c) ill adaptive sociopathy may be indicated

d) all of the above.

21/ Complete the sentence: "the glib is quintessentially....."

22/ Have you, in your private life, ever met a glib?

23/ Who appears to function socially and interpersonally?

24/ Describe the intelligence level of a typical successful psychopath.

25/ What fuels a psychopath's ability to be charismatic?

26/ Give a definition of 'charisma'?

27/ How is charisma used under a veil of affinity and morality?

28/ How does a glib achieve deception of others?

29/ Complete the following misperception of a glib: "supremely confident versus......"

30/ Also: "responsible and reliable versus....."

31/ Provide 2 other examples of charisma and how sense of entitlement

is hidden.

32/ Callousness is hidden via the glib cultivating perceptions in that

they are perceived as not having:

a) absence of empathy

b) cold-heartedness

c) absolute disregard for other's feelings

d) none of the above.

33/ Describe 2 ways in which the glib initially presents as positive to

others.

34/ What can happen with the glib (psychopath) in regards to secretive looks?

35/ How does the glib achieve a feigned positive affirmation?

36/ How does the glib perceive being observed?

37/ Which other elements (other than gestures) does the glib use to ingratiate himself/herself?

38/ Please complete the sentence: everything is a performance (by the glib) to advance:

    a) reputation

    b) needs

    c) public persona

    d) all of the above.

39/ Describe the glib's use of smug knowingness.

40/ Why does the glib use 'mirroring'?

41/ What is your understanding of 'bait and switch'?

42/ How does the glib mask aggression?

43/ Please complete the following, the glib deals with regret by:

    a) externalising it

    b) generalising it

    c) feeling great remorse

    d) a) and b).

44/ How does the glib communicate moral thought?

45/ What does the glib broaden to the wider community?

46/ Why does the glib use metaphors?

47/ Describe 3 ways in which the glib hides unemotionality.

48/ The glib's insincerity can be identified via identification of:

    a) sycophancy

    b) disloyalty

    c) feelings of superiority

    d) all of the above.

49/ Vehicles of the glib's deception include:

a) gaslighting

b) straight talking

c) propagation of lies

d) a) and c).

50/ Describe some of the ways the glib covers his/her duplicity.

51/ The glib manipulates by way of hiding that he/she is a machiavellian controller via:

a) egocentricity

b) philosophy

c) trustworthiness

d) none of the above.

52/ Which continua are relevant to glibness?

53/ What is the approximate proportion of psychopaths within the anti social personality disordered?

54/ Which individual component in addition to disinhibition is

interrelated with glibness?

55/ What emphasises the importance of identifying glibness?

56/ Complete the sentence: "one cannot be truly glib without...."

57/ How does confabulation play a part in glibness?

58/ How may one identify glibness?

59/ Glibness also involves:

a) arrogance

b) predatory approach

c) exploitation

d) all of the above.

60/ Please describe PIM.

61/ How may the glib induce others to subscribe to their ideas and

ideals?

62/ What is your understanding of a 'false sense of security'?

Provide 1 example from your personal, or work, life.

63/ The glib is:

a) perilous

b) empty inside

c) has need for greed

d) all of the above.

64/ Create your own formulaic representation of a glib's key characteristics.

65/ What is considered the umbrella term for psychopathy and sociopathy?

66/ How may one identify the difference between sociopathy and psychopathy?

67/ In which primary category does intimidation fit?

68/ Provide details of some antagonism based elements of glibness.

69/ How does disinhibition differ from antagonism (in relation to glibness)?

70/ Psychopathic features include:

a) anxiety and fear

b) social potency

c) attention seeking

d) b) and c).

71/ Please complete: 'self-entitlement is typical of....'

72/ Provide 3 characteristics of psychopathy.

73/ What is secondary psychopathy?

74/ Of principal and secondary psychopathy, which do you believe is more concerning?

75/ Which type of psychopath is more likely to experience anxiety?

76/ Why is identifying 'fearlessness' important?

77/ In your opinion, what is the difference between glib verbosity and general verbosity?

78/ Explain the juxtaposition within a chameleon-like nature.

79/ What are unexpected issues in glib children and adolescents?

80/ How is glibness realised in childhood?

81/ True or false: excellent verbal abilities are often present in a glib (antisocial) child.

82/ What can be a deciding factor in post-childhood/adolescent psychopathy?

83/ Which specific feature can manifest as meanness in conduct disorder?

84/ Describe relevant conduct disorder criteria.

85/ Limited prosocial emotions involve:

a) superficiality

b) lack of remorse

c) manipulation

d) all of the above.

86/ What is of particular concern in a child?

87/ A conduct-disordered child's lack of impulsivity is linked with...?

88/ Which factors seem unrelated to prediction of psychopathy in young adulthood?

89/ Describe some elements of the four-factor structure of psychopathy.

90/ Complete the sentence: "callous and unemotional traits are

independently present regardless of..."

91/ How are core natural rights related to glibness?

92/ Which additional features (in addition to capacity to analyse

situations) predominate in glibness?

93/ Individuals with antisocial personality disorder, are:

a) contemptuous

b) unrealistic about current problems

c) arrogantly self-appraising

d) all of the above.

94/ Lack of empathy is a feature of...?

95/ What are considered attractive qualities in some workplaces?

96/ Who often reinforces corporate psychopathy?

97/ Which type of pathology may occur in upper management?

98/ Why may a glib be attracted to specific types of work environments:

a) accolades

b) prestige

c) power

d) all of the above.

99/ (Some) Workplace cultures which encourage competitiveness also

provide.......

100/ Which factors, in addition to thriving on chaos, often impress

upper echelons (in relevant corporate environments)?

101/ What may enable the glib (psychopath) to more easily be
promoted to a higher position?

102/ How does the experience of a glib (psychopath) differ between
upper management and a co-worker?

103/ Which glib's/psychopath's characteristics may be apparent during
recruitment:

a) empathy

b) persuasiveness

c) charm

d) b) and c).

e) all of the above.

104/ What may occur when the idea of competition is introduced?

105/ Name 3 ways in which a rapid career climb can ensue.

106/ How does the psychopath behave following the orientation

(employment) phase?

107/ Provide details of other tactics (of glib/psychopath) which are

typically used... creation of toxic work culture...plus...

108/ Explain your concept of 'gaslighting'.

109/ Have you ever witnessed, or experienced, gaslighting?

110/ What can occur in workplace gaslighting?

111/ How can one minimise the chances of a glib (psychopath) being employed?

112/ Provide 2 examples of questions (regarding glibness in the workplace) which may be used in the healthcare environment.

113/ Why is it essential for assessment of glibness?

114/ What is the PCL-R?

115/ Name 1 relevant adolescent test.

116/ What is the CPTI?

117/ Name 3 areas of assessment for the CPS-R.

REFERENCES

(1a) Cleckley, H. (1988), The mask of sanity (5th ed.), St Louis, MO: Mosby,

pp. 339-340.

(1b) Dictionary.com (2023), Glibness (definition), www.dictionary.com

(2) Merriam-webster (2023), Glib (definition), www.merriam-webster.com

(3) Cleckley, H. (1976), The Mask of Sanity(4th ed), St Louis, MO: Mosby (Original work
published 1941), pp. 338-339.

(4) Oxford languages dictionary (2023), Charisma (definition),

www.oxforclearnersdictionaries.com

(5) Cambridge dictionary (2023), Charisma (definition), www.dictionary.cambridge.org

(6) Merriam- webster (2023), Charisma (definition), www.merriam-webster.com

(7) Hart, S. D. & Hare, R. D. (1996), Psychopathy and antisocial personality disorder, Current Opinion in Psychiatry, 9, 129-132.

(8) American Psychiatric Association (2022), Diagnostic and Statistical Manual of Mental Disorders, 5th ed, Text Revision: DSM-5-TR, Washington, D.C.: American Psychiatric Association Publishing, pp. 531-532; 749; 884.

(9) Lilienfeld, S. O. (2013), Is psychopathy a syndrome? Commentary on Marcus, Fulton, and Edens, Personality Disorders: Theory, Treatment, and Research, 4, 85–86.

(10) Lilienfeld, S.O. & Widows, M. R. (2005), PPI-R: Psycnopathic Personality Inventory- Revised: Professional manual, Lutz, FL: Psychological Assessment Resources.

(11) Lynam, D.R., Caspi, A., Moffitt, T.E., Loeber, R. and Stouthamer-Loebe, M. Longitudinal Evidence that Psychopathy Scores in Early Adolescence Predict Adult Psychopathy, Journal of Abnormal Psychology, 2007 February, 116(1): 155–165.

(12) Hare, R.D. (2003), Hare Psychopathy Check List- Revised (PCL-R) (2nd edn.), Toronto, Ontario, Canada: Multi-health Systems.

(13) Tophus, M.D. (2022), The Psychological Impacts of Labelling and Failure to Diagnose, Germany: Hilphma Publications; p.63.

(14) Tophus, M.D. (2023),Gaslighting, Germany: Hilphma Publications, p.23.

(15) Who is This Colleague?: Dangers of the Healthcare Profession, and beyond. An Interview Guide for Recruitment, Performance Appraisal and Post-Adverse Events. Germany: Hilphma Publications: 2022.

(16) Patrick, C.J. and Drislane, L.E., Triarchic model of psychopathy: Origins, operationalizations, and observed linkages with personality and general psychopathology, December 2015, Journal of Personality, 83 (6): 627-643.

(17a) Forth, A.E., Kosson, D.S. and Hare, R.D., (2003), The Psychopathy Check List: Youth Version, Toronto, Canada: Multi-health Systems.

(17b) Boduszek, d., Debowska, A., Dhingra, K. and Delisi, M., Introduction and validation of Psychopathic Personality Traits Scale (PPTS) in a large prison sample, Journal of Criminal Justice, 2016, 46: 9-17.

(18) Frick, P.J. and Hare, R.D. (2001), The antisocial process screening device (APSD), Toronto, Canada: Multi-health Systems

(19) Forth, A.E., Brown, S.L., Hart, S.D. and Hare, R.D. (1996), The assessment of psychopathy in male and female noncriminals: Reliability and validity, personality and individual differences, 20(5): 531-543

(20) Andershed, H., Kerr, M., Stattin, H. and Levander, S., Psychopathic traits in non-referred youths: A new assessment tool, in E. Blaauw & L. Sheridan (Eds), Psychopaths: Current international perspectives, 2002, The Hague, The Netherlands: Elsevier

(21) Collins, O.F., Andershed, H., Frogner, H., lopez-romero, L., Veen, V. and Andershed, A.K, A new measure to assess psychopathic personality in children. The child problematic traits inventory, journal of psychopathology and behavioral assessment, Journal of Psychopathology and Behavioral Assessment, 2014, 36:4-21.

(22) Lynam, D.R., Pursuing the psychopath: capturing the fledgling psychopath in a nomological net, J. Abnorm Psychol, 1997, 106:425-38